How to Look Elegant Every Day!

Colors, Makeup, Clothing, Skin & Hair, Posture and More

Elegance Series – Book 1

By

Virginia Lia

VIRGINIA LIA

How to Look Elegant Every Day! Colors, Makeup, Clothing, Skin & Hair, Posture and More

Copyright © 2017

All rights reserved. This book, or any portion thereof, may not be reproduced or used in any manner whatsoever without the express written permission from the publisher, except for the use of brief quotations in a book review.

ISBN-10: 1520253583

ISBN-13: 978-1520253589

Warning and Disclaimer

Every effort has been made to make this book as accurate as possible. However, no warranty or fitness is implied. The information provided is on an "as-is" basis. The author and the publisher shall have no liability or responsibility to any person or entity with respect to any loss or damages that arise from the information in this book.

Publisher contact

Skinny Bottle Publishing

books@skinnybottle.com

VIRGINIA LIA

Introduction

The words elegant, stylish, charming, chic, classy, and beautiful often come hand in hand. The term 'elegant' is used to describe so many people and things that it can be hard to tell what it really means. For instance, does being stylish mean being elegant? Does 'elegant' imply that you need to have the best of couture fresh from the runway?

By definition, elegance means "refined grace or restrained beauty of style". Simply put, it means any woman can have elegance and charm without the high price tag. Elegance is not just in the outfit or the way she puts makeup on, but in the way a woman carries herself – the way she talks, walks, behaves.

Some of the most elegant women in history, like Princess Diana, Grace Kelly, and Audrey Hepburn, are not just considered beautiful and elegant because they have become style icons; they are inspirational women who know how to carry themselves with grace and poise, impress with their intelligence, and win people over with their charm.

This book will show you that you do not have to be born with a silver spoon, come from royalty, become a celebrity, or date the richest guy in the world to become elegant. The book contains practical tips and tricks on how to achieve elegance without the need for stylists, a walk-in closet, or all the fancy things we think we epitomized elegance, but acted as a true liberator, designing clothing that freed women of the more classical constraints of the corset following World War I. Creating styles that allowed women to be more active, allowed them more freedom to do as they pleased; but Coco didn't stop there. An intelligent woman with lifelong drive and ambition, Coco brought her unique sense of style and aesthetics not just to clothing, but to accessories, bags, jewellery, and fragrance. Coco Chanel's signature scent, Chanel No. 5, is still a best seller today. Her legendary elegance is embodied and forever preserved in her designs, and she has been positively recognized for these contributions the world over. Her dedication to creating clothing, accessories, and fragrance that helped women embrace their elegance still stands today, making her one of the true mothers of modern elegance.

Katharine Hepburn

Certainly not the only Hepburn on the list, Katharine Hepburn embodied a type of elegance not seen by the masses before her. With finely tailored suits, crisp white shirts, and delicate, porcelain skin, Katharine Hepburn brought a classic feminine elegance to men's clothing. Hepburn fully embraced who she was as a person, following her desires, and rocking her environment with her unique sensibilities and nonconformist style. Irreverent, brilliant, and vibrant, Katharine Hepburn defined her own elegance by choosing to go against the grain, making her own way in the world with grace, poise, and embrace of the unexpected.

Lauren Bacall

Lauren Bacall is perhaps one of the finest examples of the modern elegant woman. An actress who had much more to give than what she delivered on-screen, Bacall was a force to be reckoned with, with a distinctive, smoky voice and an attitude that matched it perfectly. Bacall was one of the first to truly embody the classic 'femme fatale', earning her a spot among the icons of the film noir genre. Behind her classically sultry looks was a whip-smart, outspoken woman who strongly upheld her political beliefs, and used her position as a Hollywood film star to drive the political goals of the Democratic party. She was very active in politics, protesting the government's investigation into citizens' private political beliefs, and speaking out about policies she felt were un-American. Her unique form of elegance is evoked by intelligent, unique women who break classic molds of what it means to be a woman, and the outspoken, bold political protestors of the modern day.

Audrey Hepburn

A list of elegant women in history could never be truly complete without Audrey Hepburn. Petite, witty, and intelligent, Hepburn was committed to her status as a true role model for the modern elegant woman. Hepburn's stunning sense of style and background in ballet gave her a poised, elegant appearance, but appearance is the least of all her elegant traits. One of the top women in film of all time, Hepburn used her place in the public eye for good, working for much of her later life with UNICEF, working in some of the poorest communities in Asia, Africa, and South America to better the lives of the residents of these areas. Hepburn was awarded the Presidential Medal of Freedom for her work, solidifying her place as one of the most elegant women of all time in both appearance and in practice.

Jacqueline Kennedy Onassis

Jacqueline Kennedy Onassis, or Jackie O, is one of the first names to crop up when one thinks of elegant women, and it's easy to see why. Her classic, oft-emulated style brought the role of the First Lady to the forefront of Americans' minds, setting a standard that would be followed by all First Ladies that came after. However, it wasn't just Jackie O's style that made her an icon. She is the picture of grace and sophistication in the face of unimaginable tragedy. Kennedy Onassis suffered some of the most difficult moments a woman can face, from the loss of two of her children in infancy to a moment that changed not only her life, but the world: being seated next to her husband as he was shot. Through all of these trials, Jacqueline Kennedy Onassis held herself with grace, poise, and sophistication. Following her husband's assassination, she focused on a career in publishing and editing, proving that through even the most difficult times, there is life on the other side.

Grace Kelly

One of the best classic examples of an elegant woman, Grace Kelly, achieved the dream so many women have: becoming a princess. Kelly began her career in acting and quickly skyrocketed to fame in such films as Dial M for Murder and Rear Window, all the while making headlines for her uniquely stylish fashion choices. She was awarded the Academy Award for Best Actress for her performance in The Country Girl, solidifying her status as Hollywood royalty. Not content to stop at Hollywood royalty, Kelly later began a relationship with, and subsequently married, Prince Rainier III of Monaco, ending her acting career and beginning her life as Princess Grace. Her career, iconic fashion sense, and unique path in life etched her in the minds of all modern elegant women as a true inspiration.

These women helped define what elegance is today through their unique representation of how to be elegant. Refined, beautiful, smart, and motivated, each of them embodied elegance in their own way, inspiring generations of elegant women to follow their own path and define elegance in whatever way they choose.

Feel Elegant to Look Elegant

You've probably heard this before but it's a big truth: taking care of yourself is key. Ever wonder why the women who exude elegance and grace also have this aura of power and confidence about them? It's because they feel good about themselves, they know they deserve nothing less than being treated like a queen and they do not wait around for someone else to do it.

It starts with you. If you take care of yourself physically and emotionally, your confidence follows and it is a lot easier to look elegant despite the chaos that is going on in your life.

So while we are not going into details of how to take care of yourself emotionally, let's get right into how you can look and feel beautiful.

Elegance Basics #1: True elegance is based on a solid skincare regimen.

A good skincare regimen is key to everyday elegance. A great skincare routine doesn't have to be complicated, and can often be the difference between aging gracefully and winding up with a face full of fine lines and wrinkles. Although cosmetic procedures like Botox and fillers are available, they're pricey and can cause more problems than they solve, so before hitting the dermatologists' office, follow these simple guidelines to maintain great skin without going under the knife, or the needle.

• The basic regimen for the face is cleanse, tone, moisturize. Additional steps are to exfoliate and treat concern areas.

• Know your skin type so you can choose products accordingly. The basic types are (a) dry (b) oily (c) combination (d) sensitive/ acne prone (e) mature skin.

• Cleansing in the morning and night is what you need; over washing will cause more problems because it can strip your skin's natural oils.

• Read product labels, and as much as possible, avoid sodium lauryl sulfate.

• Use exfoliators twice a week at most. Overusing exfoliators damages the skin.

• There is wisdom in having a morning and evening moisturizer. Day moisturizers are often lighter in consistency and have SPF while night moisturizers have more restorative properties.

• Use a sunscreen that is SPF 30 and above every day. Check the label and avoid titanium dioxide and zinc oxide as much as possible.

• Pamper yourself once a week with a face mask for revitalizing the skin. Choose the ones with vitamins and antioxidants.

• Drink plenty of water for skin renewal and detoxification.

• Exercise to keep skin elasticity, flush out toxins, and counter stress (because it does show on your skin!).

• Get enough sleep.

• Maintain a healthy diet with skin food (omega 3, antioxidant rich fruits and vegetables), less alcohol and chips.

• Scrubs, or physical exfoliators, can be used up to twice a week, as they tend to be harsher on the skin. Chemical exfoliators, however, such as alpha or beta hydroxy acids like glycolic, lactic, and salicylic, can be used daily to gently exfoliate without the irritation.

• In the evening, double cleansing is essential. Double cleansing is cleansing once with a makeup removal focused cleanser and then again with your regular cleanser. The first cleanse removes surface debris while the second cleanse actually cleanses the skin.

• When using exfoliating acids, enzymes, or retinol/vitamin A, ensure that you're wearing sunscreen, as these ingredients can cause sun sensitivity.

• Cleanser and moisturizer should be suited to your skin type, while serums, masks, and treatments will suit your skin concerns. Ex. gentle cleanser and hydrating moisturizer for dry skin paired with a serum that addresses sensitivity and redness.

• Those with darker complexions should avoid physical sunscreens like titanium dioxide and zinc oxide, as these ingredients will deposit a white cast on the skin.

• For maximum benefit, use a serum. A serum is a targeted treatment product, applied before the moisturizer, that provides treatment for a specific concern- blemishes, dullness, acne, and so on.

• Taking vitamin supplements like hyaluronic acid, omega fatty acids, and niacin can improve skin health.

• Change your sheets and pillowcases at least once a week to prevent product residue and bacteria from colonizing on the skin.

• Avoid dairy and excess amounts of sugar to prevent breakouts.

Elegance Basics #2: Love your hair.

It is called your crowning glory for a reason – it is one of the first things that people see when they look at you. Hair that is well-kept and healthy-looking can show elegance even with the simplest outfit on.

• Find a haircut or hairstyle that suits your face shape.

(a) Round faces often benefit from a fuller crown and a few inches below the chin

(b) Side-swept fringe, soft curls, and layered haircuts help frame square face shapes

(c) Heart-shaped faces need ample volume and bangs to draw attention away from the pointed chin

(d) Oval face shapes can rock almost any hairstyle

• Avoid going with the trendy hairstyle. The most elegant women have wash-and-wear, easy styles.

• Avoid getting your hair done all the time. Too many chemicals and heat will damage your tresses.

• When you find a hair stylist that does your hair most beautifully, stay with that person for as long as you can. Another stylist may give you a look that is far from what you want.

• Use a shampoo that is right for your hair type. Just like our skin, the scalp can also be dry, normal or oily. There are also shampoos for a sensitive scalp, hair loss, dandruff, or color treated hair. Try a shampoo for at least a month. Changing it every week will cause damage to your hair.

• If you encounter pollution daily, washing daily may be necessary, otherwise, every other day may be okay. Too much washing will strip your tresses of oils and make them brittle, but too little will make them sticky and unhealthy.

• Comb and detangle before you wash your hair to stimulate circulation. This will greatly help when you wash.

• Wash your hair with care and do not rush it. Make sure your hair is soaked, knead your scalp and lather the shampoo before rinsing with lukewarm water.

• Never apply conditioner onto your scalp; this will irritate the follicles and weigh your hair down. Apply conditioners only to the strands and let it soak while you soap your body, shave, or sing in the shower.

• Towel dry your hair by patting and not rubbing.

• If you need to use a hair dryer, do not start at the highest setting.

• The secret to a great blow-dry is lowering the heat setting as the hair gets drier and brushing through as you go.

• Don't forget to blast the hair with cool air to avoid frizziness later on.

• Iron your hair only when it is dry.

• Thicker hair needs to be ironed longer. Remember to section the hair when ironing.

• Hair masks once a week restore your hair's shine and texture.

• An elegant or classic hair color is something that is not too far away from your original hair color. Instead of looking for a color change, opt for a shade change to get highlights or lowlights to create more dimensions rather than a drastic change.

• Even the most elegant women have bad hair days, but you never see them sporting a baseball cap to cover it all. To still look chic on a less than perfect hair day, create an updo, braid, or ponytail, then accessorize with a scarf, headband or barrette.

• Make sure to have leave-on conditioner, dry shampoo, anti-frizz serum and a paddle brush in your hair care arsenal so you can combat even the worst of hair days.

• When in doubt, a sleek bun or corporate ponytail always communicates power and confidence.

• Lengthen the time between shampoos by using a dry shampoo between washes.

• Use a heat protectant spray, cream, or serum when using heat styling tools to protect the hair from breakage, damage, and fading.

• To fight frizz on the go, rub a small amount of body/hand cream between your palms and gently smooth over any frizzy areas to instantly calm frizz.

• For those with colored hair, wash only in lukewarm water to minimize color fade, particularly for more intense shades or heavily pigmented dyes.

• To avoid breakage and split ends, sleep with a silk or satin pillowcase.

Elegance Basics #3: Mind the little details.

They say the devil is in the details. Well, in looking très chic, the smallest details matter. You will never spot the pillars of fashion and style with chipped nails or cracked heels. Here are a few pointers to remember:

• Never neglect your hands, neck, nape and arms when you wear sunscreen. These areas are prone to discoloration and wrinkling due to sun exposure.

• Don't be stingy on the exfoliant and moisturizer, especially for your hands and feet. These areas seem unnoticeable, but having hideous hands and feet is a no-no for elegant ladies.

• Great nails need to be filed nicely so don't file while you are doing something else. If you can afford to get a mani-pedi often, go for it. Otherwise, doing it at home is pretty easy as long as you can focus.

(a) The classic nail shapes are oval and square. Do not go for an almond shape because it looks less formal and is considered more for costume-y events.

(b) Classic nail colors are nudes and soft pinks. Opt for red if you want to call for a little attention without being over the top. Save jewel tones as seasonal colors. Leave the candy colors and neons to the younger girls.

(c) Avoid nail art, metallic colors, and anything that is trendy since they tend to look cheap.

(d) For a graceful look even for the shortest and stubbiest of fingers, simply avoid colors too bright or dark. Bright, deep shades accentuating the ends of the fingers can cause the hands to appear smaller and fingers to appear shorter.

(e) Beautiful nails aren't just well-maintained nail beds; soak hands and remove any excess dead skin from the cuticles by lightly scrubbing each finger before painting the nails.

(f) When searching for the perfect hand cream, look for creams that serve as both nourishing hand hydrators and as nail treatment creams. Consistent hydration of the hands is key to an elegant appearance, and working at nail nourishment will help you maintain strong, healthy nails, keeping them perfect through every new shade of polish.

• When it comes to getting the perfect smile, aside from the obvious regular brushing, flossing, and using a mouthwash, you may want to:

(a) Have regular cleanings at the dentist to take care of plaque and stains.

(b) A quick tip is to mix baking soda with your regular toothpaste and brush with this once a week to get rid of some stains on your teeth.

(c) Use a straw when drinking coffee, tea, or juices to avoid stains.

(d) Brush a little longer than usual.

• When choosing pieces to tie your look together, choose the ones that add a pop of color and refinement without going overboard. A flash of gold detailing or a dash of leopard is chic; a full, heavily patterned look is not.

• Use those small pops of color to make a statement. You may love fire engine red, but a full red ensemble is a little much- choosing a statement shoe, necklace, or bag is much more effective than overdoing your look.

Elegance Basics #4: Posture perfect.

Good posture has a lot to do with exuding confidence, while affecting bone alignment, muscle tone, etc. People with good posture when walking, standing and sitting, look and feel better. Luckily, good posture is more nurture than nature — meaning, with ample practice and making it a habit, it is possible to stand tall and confident no matter what your height or body type is.

So what does good posture mean? Good posture means having a straight line from the earlobes through the shoulders, down to the hips, knees, and ankles when you are standing up. Basically, it means having the spine in alignment. By no means does alignment mean just plain straight because our spine is not naturally straight. Have you seen those beauty queens walking straight or standing up so straight? Nope. Good posture means simply standing, sitting or walking without slouching or ducking your head – as if your spine is reaching for something up over your head (if you can picture that).

• Exercise and stretching help with good posture, and build muscle tone.

• A strong core and strong calves are essential to having great posture.

• You don't need to imagine walking on a line just to have good posture. Don't march, don't be stiff. A steady gait and easy glide-like walk will suffice.

• Make sure to have lumbar support when you are sitting down. If your chair does not have a curve that matches your back, sit up straight or use a pillow for support.

• When you walk, your weight should be on the balls of your feet and not your heels.

• When you stand, your feet should always be shoulder width apart so that there will not be too much pressure on your back.

• If you need to stand for photos, though, a good trick is to momentarily cross one foot at one ankle or put one foot in front of the other slightly.

• Still not sure what to do? Stand next to a wall without leaning or pushing on it. The back of your head, your shoulders, and your buttocks are the only parts touching the wall. This is what a good standing and walking posture looks like. With practice, it can become second nature to you!

• Remember that your sitting posture affects your standing posture so don't sit for too long in one day. The same is true for driving posture. Aside from making sure your sitting position is comfortable, you also have to check that your spine is in alignment and you are not slouching.

• Although it does not seem to matter as much, having good sleeping posture can affect the quality of your sleep and the way your body feels when you wake up. If you sleep on your back, try putting a pillow behind your knees. If you sleep on your side, put the pillow between your knees. Align your spine with a pillow or two if you must.

Know Your Colors

When learning how to be elegant, it is vital to learn to work with what you have. Now that we have tackled the important bit about taking care of your body, we move on to yet another body-related issue. This time we will delve into knowing your colors. Knowledge of spotting your undertones and embracing your colors is important so that you can bring out the best in you as you choose makeup and clothing.

Here's the thing, no matter how expensive or stylish the clothes, accessories, hair and makeup are, they are not going to suit each and every one of us. What looks good on your style icon or your favorite celebrity may not necessarily work for you. Ladies, you already know that we come in all shapes, sizes, and colors. The most elegant people know how to choose colors (for fashion and styling) based on their skin color, eye color, and even their hair color so that these do not clash.

So it's not really about picking the Pantone color of the year, or going with what's hot on the red carpet or catwalk. Not yet convinced? Check out the benefits of knowing your colors:

• Learning to spot which colors accentuate your best features will make shopping, getting dressed, and going to the salon much, much easier.

• Mismatched colors can make or break a look. Even if the clothes are pretty, they can still make you look dull, matronly, or trying too hard.

• Knowing how to mix and match your best colors can help you create looks that hide your problem areas, or make you look slimmer, curvier, or more athletic, however you please.

Ready to get started? Okay, here we go.

1) Skin Tone

First up is knowing your skin tone. You can either be warm, cool or neutral. Here are ways to find out:

• Check the veins on your wrists and arms. If they're more blue or purple, your skin tone is cool. If you have more green than blue veins, you're warm. If it's a mix of blue and green then you're a neutral or olive.

• Observe the glow of your skin under natural light. If you appear pink, you have a cool undertone. If you appear yellowish or peachy, you have a warm undertone. If you look a bit in between then you are a neutral or olive undertone.

• Think about the way your skin reacts in the absence of sunscreen. If your skin tends to tan easily, you are warm. If your skin tends to turn red or burn, you are cool, and if your skin burns then heals into a tan, you're olive or neutral.

A. Warm Skin Tones

-looks most elegant in the shades of fire and earth like reds, oranges, yellows and browns

-looks best with gold accessories

-opt for peach or berry shades for lipsticks and blushes

-when wearing nude colors opt for off-whites or golden undertones

B. Cool Skin Tones

-looks most elegant in the colors of the sky or the bottom colors of the rainbow like greens, blues, and purples

-looks best with silver accessories

-true pink and purplish lipsticks and blushes work best

C. Neutral or Olive Skin Tones

-can wear pretty much any color

-look better in bronze or gold accessories

2) Hair Color

Choosing outfit colors based on hair color is less important than the skin tone. However, it is good to know which colors suit your hair color best when choosing a top. Since your blouse will be closest to your hair, it pays to know this bit. For example, if you are a redhead, it does not mean that reds and pinks are total no-nos. It only means that you would be better off wearing the reds and pinks as bottoms than tops.

A. Brown or Black Hair – with white, black, pastels, red, pink, yellow, jeweled blue

B. Blonde Hair – earth tones, navy blue, orange, peach, jeweled green

C. Red Hair – browns and earth colors, light greens, light blues, and muted golds

3) Mixing and Matching Using the Color Wheel

Get yourself a color wheel from a bookstore or print one from online. Now let's learn about the different color schemes you can use to mix and match:

A. Complimentary Color Scheme – two colors placed opposite each other on the wheel (e.g. red and green, yellow and purple)

B. Analogous Color Scheme – three adjacent colors belonging to the same color family, often found in nature together

C. Triadic Color Scheme – 3 colors, evenly spaced out in the color wheel (e.g. yellow, orange, blue)

• White, black, brown, gray, green and blue are considered neutral colors that go with almost anything. Generally, you can look elegant with any of these neutral colors plus a pop of an accent color, which you will base on your skin tone, hair color, and the color wheel.

• Use the color schemes above to effectively color block when you want to use more than the neutral+1 accent color formula. But this is not to say use all bright shades of the color schemes at the same time. Elegance means striking a good balance in your use of color. For example, use the analogous color scheme by wearing dark blue jeans, dark purple heels, a white top, and a blue violet statement necklace.

• Wear dark colors on areas you want to slim down, and brighter or lighter colors on areas you want to accentuate. For example, make hips look less wide with darker skirts.

• Wear similar colors of bottoms and shoes to elongate the legs.

General tips on colors:

• Aside from matching the colors with your skin tone, hair color, and knowledge of the color wheel, consider the seasons too. A pop of color during rainy or gloomy weather always looks chic.

• Neutrals are classic elegant pieces that can be worn all over. They are almost as sophisticated as black. Monochromatic dressing a la Audrey Hepburn is always a good idea.

• Never pair black outfits with heavy black eyeliner.

• Deep colors are always more flattering, and classier looking than pastels.

• Remember to look at the colors in the patterns of your clothes too.

• Follow the rule of three – use a maximum of three colors for your entire ensemble so you do not look like kindergarten artwork.

Embrace Your Shape

A big part of looking elegant is dressing according to your body shape and body type. Even the most high-end brands look unsightly on people who do not consider the right fit. If it's too tight, or too loose, it makes you look short or just plain oddly proportioned; no one will care if it's Gucci, Armani or Dior. With so many style and fabric options out there, it is really hard to pick outfits that will look great on you.

So this is where taking stock of your physical attributes and embracing your shape comes in. There are generally 4 body shapes that fall into 2 body types. Take a look:

Athletic

Characteristics: looks slender, toned and angular with small hips, sharp shoulders, and a broad frame

Body Shape: ruler, the body shape of almost all runway models

Best Looks:

• Light fabrics to soften angles (e.g. silk, chiffon, wool)

- Girly or frilly embellishments such as ruffles, puffed sleeves, bows

- Empire waist, peasants tops to create the illusion of a bust area

- Flaunt legs in shorts and skirts

- Peplum skirts give the illusion of wider hips

- Flared skirts that add more shape

- Accessorize with statement necklaces and brooches for the illusion of a bigger bust

- Peep-toed shoes with strappy details emphasize your killer legs

- A-line cocktail dresses, mermaid gowns with volume, and feminine details

Avoid:

- Manly tops (e.g. military-inspired, button-up shirts)

- Bermuda shorts

Curvy

Characteristics: round shoulders with hips and bust flaring out

Body Shapes:

- Hourglass – generally considered as the ideal physique because of the proportion of hips and bust

- Pear – curves starting from the waist are larger than shoulder and chest area

• Apple – shoulder and chest area is wider than the hips

Best Looks:

• Tailored outfits (e.g. with button-up, lapels, folds)

• Tops that hug the waist

• V-neck tops that draw attention to the bust line and make the torso appear longer

Apple: capris, A-line or flare skirts, sleek stilettos or nude pumps, off-shoulder tops, fitted waist

Pear: dark bottoms, light top, boat collars, scoop or off-shoulder neckline, corseted bodice, sweetheart neckline, pumps, wedges, boots

Hourglass: tops that accentuate the waist, pencil cut skirt, fitted tops with high necklines, light colored dresses

Avoid:

• Adding more curves

• Empire waist that makes you look pregnant

• Baggy jeans

Basic Tips:

• When in doubt, go for A-lines, straight leg trousers, and sheath dresses. They flatter almost all shapes and body types.

• Again, elegant women choose simple classics over trendy ones.

• Try clothes on before you buy them. Alterations cost extra and are only advisable for those who are extra tall or petite.

• Choose clothes that fit you in the here and now. If it's too small or too big, you're probably not going to wear it again.

• Pay attention to the hemline, shoulders, crotch area, pleats and zippers too when you fit.

Elegance is also about comfort. So aside from getting clothes that really fit you well, you also have to consider that the clothes have to be comfortable and pleasing to you above all else. Even if the high heels and blazer combo looks elegant and stylish, if you feel horrible in it, you will not carry it well. People will see your pain instead of the elegance you are trying to achieve.

Another important piece of dressing for your body is taking your height into consideration. Tall women can wear styles that simply don't work on shorter frames, and vice versa, so when dressing for your size, take your height into consideration and keep these tips in mind.

Tall

• Tall women have more space to rock a bold print, so don't shy away from colorful looks or patterned statement pieces.

• For larger, flowing pieces, add a belt to your natural waist to define your shape and balance your look.

• For pant legs or sleeves that are too short, own that cropped look by cuffing them to create a more intentional look.

• Balance your look with accessories that coordinate and tie your look together from head to toe. This creates a more cohesive, pulled-together look.

• Embrace your height by rocking pieces that enhance and emphasize it, like jumpsuits and maxi dresses.

• Wear heels that are only 3 inches tall, max.

• For winter weather, embrace long line coats or a knee-length trench to keep warm rather than a more cropped, puffy jacket, as this will create a top-heavy, unflattering look.

• Stick with mid-rise to high-rise jeans and pants, as low-rise will generally not have nearly enough height to appropriately cover a longer torso.

• Avoid anything boxy with heavy, large shoulders or shoulder pads to avoid appearing too top-heavy.

• Check clothing care instructions before washing; shrinkage for a tall girl can ruin a perfect piece.

Short

• Lengthening your look is key for shorter women, so avoid horizontal lines in your clothing patterns.

• Skip shoes with ankle straps. This cuts the leg off at the ankle and makes legs appear shorter and stumpier.

• Dress up any outfit by adding a pair of nude heels that match your skin tone. This gives the legs a naturally elongated look, whether you're wearing a dress, skirt, or pants.

• Make outfits appear more tailored and refined by tucking in looser tops at the center, letting the rest hang out. This half-tuck helps add structure to an otherwise baggy look.

• To avoid pants looking too long, cuff them just below the ankle.

• Define a loose-fitting dress by adding a belt at the waist.

• Avoid wearing too many pieces at once- an already small frame will be overwhelmed by too much clothing. Choose only key pieces, and avoid too many layers, large, bulky scarves, or more than two pieces of jewelry.

• Choose pieces, like jackets and blazers, that fall at the natural waist or just below the rear. Lengths in between tend to emphasize a short stature.

• Ensure any looser-fitting clothing is balanced with a more form-fitting piece to avoid getting swallowed up by your outfit. Ex. A loose fitting top paired with fitted leggings or pants.

• Avoid large, clunky shoes that will unbalance your look.

Wardrobe 101

First impressions really count. People tend to make judgments based on what they see, so it is always a good idea to spend some time learning how to dress your best with a few basic pieces. Keep in mind what we've already tackled colors and shapes before you proceed, okay? And oh, everything from the list of 10 wardrobe essentials are investment pieces that you should consider investing in.

1. Little Black Dress

We have Coco Chanel to thank for the popularity of the LBD! This is a timeless piece that flatters all skin tones and body types. It is also easy to wear for various occasions. It can be dressed up or dressed down depending on how you would accessorize, do your hair and makeup. Here are a few formulations that feature the versatile LBD:

• Corporate Event = LBD + killer heels + dress watch + simple earrings + red lipstick + high ponytail or bun

• Date Night = LBD + nice earrings + shoes or wedges + simple makeup

• Family Party = LBD + cute shoes or sneakers + cozy jacket

• Makeup should enhance, not mask you. It should highlight your features while drawing less attention on your flaws.

• Choose your makeup color from your skin's undertones.

• Great skin is the best makeup base, so take care of it.

• Just like skincare, your makeup should match your skin type so you won't risk getting irritations.

• Keep shimmers to a minimum especially if you will be wearing accessories on your head. You don't want to look like a disco ball.

Makeup Kit Essentials:

• A good skincare routine. Great makeup starts with great skin, so ensure skin is properly cleansed and moisturized before makeup application.

• Primer. A face primer is essential to makeup that lasts all day long, so choose a primer that suits your skin type. Apply all over the face and down the neck before applying makeup.

• Concealer. A great concealer is essential to minimize undereye darkness, blemishes, and an uneven skin tone.

• Foundation. Your foundation is essential to creating a beautiful complexion. Use only as much as needed to avoid a cakey look. Choose a foundation that matches you shade-wise as closely as possible in whatever texture works best for your skin type (liquid, powder, and so on).

• Blush. Blush defines the cheekbones and livens up the complexion, helping you avoid a look that's flat and non-dimensional.

• Eyebrow pencil. Well-defined brows are essential for framing the face, so choose a fine-tipped, freshly sharpened brow pencil to define your eyebrows.

• A good, everyday lipstick. Lips, like brows, help to frame the face and complete your look by pulling it together. Choose a shade that resembles your natural lips, but with a rosier tone to emphasize lips in a natural way.

• Mascara. Eyelashes are the last step to defining and framing the face. Choose either a basic black or a black-brown shade and apply two coats to define the lashes.

• Eye makeup remover. Whether it's for small touch-ups during application or full removal at the end of the day, a good eye makeup remover is key to ensure no residue is left behind on the eyes that may irritate them.

For a night out, you may want a more dramatic look. Some great ways to amp up your look for the evening include:

• Apply your eye makeup first in your makeup routine: after primer, but before complexion makeup. This helps minimize smudging and eyeshadow fall-out ruining the complexion.

• For eyes, avoid a look too heavy on dark shades. Keep deeper shades to the outer corner and the crease of the eyelid rather than the full lid to maintain a dimensional, classic look that's not overdone.

• When using eyeliner, apply as close to the lash line as possible.

• For a long-lasting lip look, apply lip liner around the outer edges and continue to fill in the entire area of the lip with the liner as well. This helps your lip look grip better to the lips and last through drinks, dinner, and conversation.

natural look, opt for a basic mascara in a black/brown shade rather than full, intense black.

• To naturally enhance lips, apply lip liner that's closest to the natural shade of the lip all over the full lip area to provide an even color. Heavily outlined lips that remain nude in the center are too dramatic for every day.

Key Makeup Mistakes To Avoid

• Ensure your complexion products are properly matched. An improperly matched foundation can be the difference between natural elegance and an obviously made-up look. Know your undertones, and choose a foundation that not only matches those but is closest in shade to your natural skin.

• Apply concealer sparingly- a heavy amount of concealer is more obvious than you think, and can actually emphasize, rather than hide, any imperfections.

• Choose products meant for your skin type. A heavy, matte finish foundation on dry skin is a total disaster. Choose products that work well with your skin to create the most natural look possible.

• If your skin is dry, use powder sparingly. Powder can cause a look to become heavy, and for those with fine lines, wrinkles, and uneven texture, powder emphasizes these features.

• When applying liner, ensure it is applied as close to the lash line as possible, but avoid applying a liner look that is simply a harsh line all the way around the eye. This creates the illusion of a smaller eye, which defeats the eye-opening properties your liner has in the first place.

• Avoid applying mascara too heavily to bottom lashes. This can dramatically unbalance your look and make you look way too made-up.

• Choose a blush shade that naturally flushes the face, and blends well - stark, unblended blush is an easy way to rock a clown-like look.

• Ensure your key features are defined; brows, lips, and lashes. Over-emphasizing any of these while forgoing the others will cause the face to appear unfinished.

• Use a lip liner with any heavily pigmented lip product. Lack of lip liner will allow your lip color to bleed out past the lip line, smudge, and be a nuisance throughout the day overall.

• Use a light hand when applying bronzer. This keeps your look from veering out of healthy bronzed territory into a chalky, over-tanned look.

Fragrance:

• Elegant scents are fresh and natural. Scents that are too sweet or too heavy tend to smell cheap.

• Choosing a fragrance is a highly personal thing and only people who get close to you will get a whiff, so make sure to make it memorable but not overpowering.

• Do not mix too many scents at once. It's a better idea to have similar scents for your hair products, shower products, and perfume. Layering these products will also make sure you smell good for a longer period of time.

• Spray a cloud of perfume in the air and pass through it so you get just the right amount of scent on you.

• If you want to have a scent stay on longer, dab a small amount of fragrance directly on your temples and wrists.

• When applying fragrance, do not rub the wrists together; this will break down the fragrance and keep it from lasting all day long. Simply dab on the area and press wrists together to push the fragrance into the skin.

• Apply your fragrance to key pulse points for maximum wear time. The nape of the neck, wrists, inner elbows, back of the knees, and decolletage are key areas to apply fragrance to ensure it lasts as long as possible.

• Having a signature scent is key to elegance. Scent is the strongest sense tied to memory, and a truly elegant woman is unforgettable- just like her scent. Choose an everyday fragrance that works from day to night for your signature scent that doesn't dip off into extremes- too musky, too floral, or too sweet. More intense scents are best reserved for special occasions.

• When heading off on vacation, or for a special event, carefully choose your fragrance. This fragrance will forever remind you of this moment in time, and just a whiff can take you back to the sultry summer days or warm winter nights on which you first wore it. Use fragrances to create a long-lasting statement.

-casual: sundress or nice blouse, skirt or pants

Quick guide to dress codes

I cannot stress this enough, being elegant means not just dressing nicely, but appropriately. Here's a quick guide to the occasions and the dos and don'ts for each:

1. Weddings

Don't:

• Wear something that will upstage the bride, her wedding party, or the mothers.

• Wear jeans unless the theme calls for it.

• Wear the exact color of the motif.

Do:

• Match your outfit with the season, the location, the wedding theme and your role.

• If you are invited to the ceremony you might need to dress more conservatively for places of worship.

• Ask the bride or the ladies of the wedding party if you may wear your LBD. This can save you some shopping time and will make you stand out from the usual sea of pastels and jewel tones others are likely to wear.

• Leave the sparkles to the bride and her bridal party. Opt for understated jewelry instead.

• Day weddings usually call for light fabrics in pastel colors

• Jewel tones and deeper colors are usually for night weddings.

2. Job Interview (also works for corporate events)

Don't:

• Look like you are going on a date or a workout

• Wear perfume to lessen risks of distracting others

• Wear flashy jewelry, dangling earrings, and bracelets that make noise

Do:

• Opt for a classic and crisp suit in traditional firms and offices. It is the safest option.

• Check the company's website first to know what the work environment is like. More creative companies do not have a dress code, so you may go in business casual with a creative focal point.

• Consider the position you are applying for. You have to look the part.

• Keep your arms covered with three-quarter or long sleeves.

• Skirts and dresses should always be a little below the knee, in solid colors or minimal geometric patterns.

• Keep these in mind: tailored, smooth and neat.

• Wear understated, natural makeup.

• Bring a professional bag and a notepad.

3. First Date

Don't:

• As they always say, "Dress to impress."

• Wear an outfit you have never worn before. You might end up with an uncomfortable feeling, or a wardrobe malfunction.

• Wear something that shows too much skin. Leaving too little to the imagination is never elegant.

Do:

• Dress comfortably. Wear something you would normally wear.

• If you need to be in a dress, your LBD, a wrap dress or sheath dress should be good to go.

4. Dinner Gatherings

• Dress to the nines, especially when you are seated at the VIP.

• Opt for your LBD, long dress, or an evening clutch.

• If you must go in jeans, make sure they are dark and not frayed. Pair them with a dressy top and nice jewelry.

This list is by no means exhaustive, but if you follow these recommendations, you will be on the road to looking elegant all the time.

Etiquette

Elegance isn't all about looks. Your behavior and the way you carry yourself are major contributors to how you present yourself to others. These simple steps will help you present your most elegant self without having to alter a thing about your appearance.

Timeliness.

In any situation, being on time is key. Your arrival in a timely fashion to an interview, party, or event makes a key statement about who you are as a person; organized, thoughtful, and understanding of others' time constraints. Maintaining timeliness includes adding 20 minutes to your initial commute time in the event you have difficulty finding parking, or get lost.

Maintain Good Manners.

Proper manners are key in any situation, but in our modern times, it can be difficult to navigate how exactly to best go about maintaining proper manners. Some tips for good manners that never go out of style include:

• Keeping your voice/phone/etc at a healthy volume. Maintaining appropriate volume levels shows poise and elegance.

• Always be sure to introduce yourself to new people as soon as you meet them, and introduce any guests you have with you as well. When everyone in a situation has been properly introduced to each other, it creates a more comfortable environment for everyone involved.

• Make an effort to help in a situation in which it seems that another person is struggling, within reason. Take the temperature of the situation before going forward, but when appropriate, help others carry bags, hold doors, and do whatever small tasks need to be done to help another person.

• Respectfully regard the other person in any situation by maintaining comfortable levels of personal space and avoid making the person/people you're with feel trapped by too much interaction, or backing them into a corner, either literally or figuratively.

• Never leave a gathering without saying goodbye to the host or the person who invited you. This shows your appreciation for the invite and your appreciation for their company.

Professionalism In The Workplace

Proper workplace etiquette is key when it comes to presenting an elegant appearance. In the workplace, be sure to:

• Adhere to workplace policies regarding timeliness, relationships with coworkers, and general behavior.

• Never enter a room without knocking.

• Ensure that any important communication is either written down and delivered by hand, or e-mailed within a timely fashion. Word of mouth communication is easily forgotten, can make it seem as though your communication isn't important, and can put undue stress on your superiors.

• Respect boundaries of time on the clock vs. off the clock. If your issue isn't an emergency, it can likely wait until a time when you and your coworkers are on the clock to deal with it.

• Minimize phone calls to short, pressing issues rather than constant long-winded calls. This shows a respect for the time of the person you're communicating with.

• Avoid being too familiar with new supervisors. Treat every new business relationship with respect.

• Behave respectfully at any after-work function, and generally avoid having more than two drinks, regardless of the behavior of others in the workplace. They may be comfortable with potentially embarrassing themselves, but you should maintain professionalism.

• Always respond to requests or communication given in the morning by the conclusion of the business day. Respond to requests given in the afternoon by the end of the day if possible, but ensure that all requests from the previous day are taken care of early the following day at the latest.

• Keep your temper in check. Though workplace stressors may seem impossible to quietly deal with at times, maintaining an even attitude and avoiding explosive conflict will benefit you far more than losing your temper or shouting.

• Stay quiet regarding trash talk at work. If someone is speaking ill of someone else to you, there's a good chance they're speaking ill of you to someone else. Disengage yourself from conversations that turn to workplace gossip. You may not want to appear unsympathetic or uncaring, but gossip or trash talk in the workplace rarely leads to anything positive. Keep your head down and do your job as best you can.

Social Etiquette

Knowing how to behave in a social setting is key to an elegant appearance. Those with proper social etiquette are able to truly maximize their interactions and create sustainable, long-lasting friendships and relationships. These tips will help you go above and beyond to showcase your elegance in any social situation.

• Keep your engagements. When planning social engagements, ensure that you will have the time, stamina, and focus to successfully attend any social gathering before agreeing to attend. If you honestly feel that you will not be able to attend due to an emergency, calling the host or the person who invited you goes much further in others' minds than a text. Canceling plans via text is almost never acceptable, particularly for individuals who you don't already know well.

• When you receive an RSVP, always reply. Not replying is not an acceptable way to indicate you are not attending an event. Always ensure you reply to RSVP's in a timely fashion, whether you plan on attending or not, and be sure to honestly reply; if you're not sure you will be able to attend, indicate that in your reply.

• For gifts, a handwritten thank you note goes miles. A simple verbal thank you shows gratitude, but a handwritten note shows you truly care and value the person who gave the gift.

• When it comes to birthdays, milestones, or rough times in the lives of close friends, if you cannot be there in person, a phone call is the best way to show you care. Ensuring they hear your voice to wish them well goes much further in our minds than a simple text or a birthday wish online.

• If a friend or a family member has a registry for their wedding or baby shower, do your best to purchase from the registry. They've taken the time to indicate the things they need, so you should also take the time to ensure you're providing those items. If you have a great gift idea that falls outside the scope of the registry, don't simply offer that item; choose at least one item from the registry, while also presenting your own thoughtful gift. This shows you care while also showing you went above and beyond to find the perfect items for them.

• If a friend or family member requests a courtesy text or call before you arrive at their event/to pick them up/etc., ensure you provide that communication in a timely fashion. No one likes to be surprised by a guest before they're ready!

• Respect boundaries. Not everyone goes about friendships and relationships the same, so if you feel you may be overstepping a boundary in any situation, proceed with caution or rethink your approach. You may wind up doing more harm than good.

Restaurant Etiquette

When dining out, proper restaurant etiquette makes the experience more enjoyable for yourself, your party, and the waitstaff. Follow these tips to make your evening out more pleasant for everyone involved.

• Allow the person closest to the waiter to order first. This helps the staff organize who gets what item and allows everyone to order in a comfortable, sensible fashion.

• Wait until everyone has received their entree to begin eating.

• Ensure you're sitting up straight, maintaining good posture, and avoid leaning your body or your elbows on the table.

• Mind your volume when eating. No one likes to hear chomping, slurping, or really any noise coming out of your mouth when there's also food in it. Chew with your mouth closed to minimize any noise, and eat slowly.

• At a meal where you are a guest and won't be paying, try to keep your choices at a lower cost rather than ordering the most expensive meal, and stick to items you know you'll be able to finish. Leaving a large quantity of food when you aren't paying can appear insulting to some.

• When at dinner, no matter how large your party, put your phone away and place your focus on your companions. If you must send a text or take a call, try your best to do so away from the table so as not to interrupt the conversation with your own personal discussion.

• At the conclusion of the meal, always tip. Whether the service was top notch or not, tipping is part of the restaurant world, and you should figure in the cost of the tip when deciding to dine out.

Etiquette is key to elegance. Keep those tips in mind to bring elegance to every interaction, every day.

Conclusion

So what does it take to become elegant? It takes being the total package, being elegant from the inside out; it's being confident, graceful and kind; it's being wise to know how to be appropriate and still fun the right amounts.

Win a free

kindle
OASIS

Let us know what you thought of this book to enter the sweepstake at:

reviewers.win/lookelegant